The Endless Possibilities
with
Nora & Vincent

By Nigel Marcellus
Illustrated by Bryant Billue

Edited by
Valerie Lowe-Barehmi
and Chanel Friday

"Anything is possible for those who believe!"

One day while watching TV,
Vincent saw his
favorite basketball players,
football players, and musical artist!

He imagined himself
shooting the game winning shot,
scoring a touchdown
in the Super Bowl,
and performing on a stage
in front of thousands of people.

Vincent ran outside
excited to
do it all!

First, he tried
to shoot a basketball,
but he missed the shot.

Next, he grabbed a football and ran, but the ball fell out of his hands.

Then he tried to sing,
but he did not like
how he sounded.

Sad, because he couldn't
be like the people he watched on TV,
Vincent went home.
Nora was there waiting for Vincent
and saw that he was upset.

"What's wrong?"- Nora asked.

"I give up!
I'm not good at basketball,
football, or singing."
-Vincent cried.

"You have to practice and
work for your goals silly!
Follow me, I'll show you!"
-Nora said.

Nora shot the basketball
and missed the first.

She kept shooting
and finally made one!

Nora then tried
to score a touchdown
but kept dropping the football.

Eventually, she ran
for a touchdown
without dropping the football!

Then Nora
began to sing.

**After singing
the song over and over,
she began to sound wonderful.**

"Wow!"-Vincent said.
"See, just because you don't succeed the first time doesn't mean you can't do it."
- Nora explained.

"Could you and I
become those people on TV?"
-Vincent asked.

"I could and so could you!"
- Nora said.

"We can also become
scientists, business owners,
police officers, astronauts or
construction engineers.
There's so much out there
for us to be!"
- Nora explained.

"How can I
be one of them?"
-Vincent asked.

"My parents tell me
if you have a dream,
work hard and never give up;
you will become it!"
– Nora explained.

"If I can do it, you can too!
I won't stop dreaming
because anything is possible!"
– Nora said.

Vincent's imagination
begins to run wild...

**"Thanks for reading!
Take care until our next adventure."**

-Nigel Marcellus & Bryant Billue

Made in United States
North Haven, CT
05 January 2024

47101751R00024